S0-DOQ-445

# a slip of the tongue

## Offhand Remarks That Derailed High-Powered Careers

By Joel Fram and Sandra Salmans

RUNNING PRESS
PHILADELPHIA · LONDON

© 2005 by Running Press
All rights reserved under the Pan-American and International Copyright Conventions
Printed in the United States

*This book may not be reproduced in whole or in part, in any form or by any means, electronic
or mechanical, including photocopying, recording, or by any information storage and retrieval
system now known or hereafter invented, without written permission from the publisher.*

9   8   7   6   5   4   3   2   1
Digit on the right indicates the number of this printing

Library of Congress Control Number: 2005901967

ISBN-13: 978-0-7624-2494-8
ISBN-10: 0-7624-2494-X

Cover and interior illustrations by Richard Beckerman
Cover and interior design by Alicia Freile
Edited by Michael Tomolonis and Jennifer Kasius

This book may be ordered by mail from the publisher.
Please include $2.50 for postage and handling.
***But try your bookstore first!***

Running Press Book Publishers
125 South Twenty-second Street
Philadelphia, Pennsylvania 19103-4399

Visit us on the web!
www.runningpress.com

*"I have noticed that nothing I never said ever did me any harm."*
—Calvin Coolidge

A man of few words, President Coolidge never had to apologize for anything he ever—or never—said. Maybe the people in this book should have followed Silent Cal's example.

But they didn't. In fact, they couldn't stop talking until their feet were planted firmly in their mouths. Some of the brightest careers in politics, sports and business have been snuffed out or seriously jeopardized with a few ill-chosen words. Many of these remarks achieved national notoriety; in other cases, the humiliation was strictly local. In each case, the speaker abandoned discretion just long enough to universally rankle sensibilities and foment loud calls for resignation.

Why are some careers destroyed by a few words while others survive? That often has as much to do with *who* is doing the talking as what is said. In case you're concerned about your own slips of the tongue, we offer a few guidelines.

Snobbery gets you snubbed—especially if you're turning up your nose at the people you need. English jeweler Gerald Ratner learned this. So did one-time gubernatorial candidate Ed Koch and onetime queen Marie Antoinette.

Remarks that reveal you to be mean-spirited, unpatriotic or hypocritical fall flat. So do remarks in overtly bad taste, such as wisecracks about 9/11 or the deadly 2004 tsunami.

The sort of racism, sexism and homophobia that was expressed openly within recent memory is now highly suspect—unless, perhaps, if it comes from a member of a group more oppressed than the one disparaged. In other words, if you're a rich, straight, white guy, watch your mouth.

If you're a sitting President or Vice President, you have less to worry about than others in the public eye. Publishers have printed whole books of laughable remarks by Ronald Reagan, Dan Quayle and George W. Bush. But nothing they said cost them an election.

We think you'll find the quotations in this book and their consequences to be lively reading—and a reminder that even the highest-and-mightiest can do themselves in with a few unfortunate words. You're sure to be relieved that *you* didn't say *that*—and oddly happy that someone else did.

# Let Whoopi Be Whoopi? Maybe Not

• • •

Her fans love Whoopi Goldberg's raunchy brand of humor. But a fundraiser for the 2004 Democratic presidential ticket might have been the wrong gig for her X-rated patter.

At a star-studded concert at New York's Radio City Music Hall that raised $7.5 million, Whoopi noted that she'd been asked to submit her monologue in advance. Instead, "I Xeroxed my behind and I folded it up in an envelope and I sent it back with a big kiss mark," she boasted.

"Because we're Democrats. We don't do that. We're not afraid to laugh. That's the other people."

Then she grabbed her genitals. "I love bush," she said. **"But someone's giving bush a bad name. . . . Someone has waged war, someone has deliberately misled the country, someone has attempted to amend the Constitution all in the name of Bush . . . My bush is smarter than that. And if my bush is smarter than that, you can understand just how dumb I think that other bush is. . . . I will do whatever it takes to restore bush to its rightful place and that ain't in the White House. Vote your heart and mind and keep bush where it belongs."**

The hush from the audience, some of whom had paid $25,000 apiece for the gala, wasn't what Goldberg expected. "This is what I try to explain to people," she said. "Why are you asking me to come if you don't want me to be me?"

We're not asking, replied Slim-Fast, the diet drink company that had hired Whoopi as its spokesperson "because of her commitment to losing weight." The company promptly announced it was firing her because her monologue "does not reflect the views and values of Slim-Fast." Clearly, Slim-Fast's interest in Whoopi's anatomy didn't extend to her private parts.

# Rush to Judgment

● ● ●

In September 2003, millions of listeners heard conservative radio haranguer Rush Limbaugh declare on ESPN that **"the media has been very desirous that a black quarterback do well,"** and that Philadelphia Eagles quarterback Donovan McNabb **"got a lot of credit for the performance of this team that he didn't deserve."** A few days later, Limbaugh resigned from ESPN amid speculation that he had been forced out for his impolitic remarks. An ESPN commentator

who was on the show with Limbaugh remarked that his "comments made us uncomfortable."

Anybody who thought that Limbaugh suffered for telling the truth about McNabb had only to follow the quarterback's career for the next few months. On the day that Limbaugh disparaged his talents, McNabb led the Eagles to their first victory of the season over the Buffalo Bills. As the season progressed, he was instrumental in leading the Eagles to clinch the NFC East title. He was named NFC offensive player for November and selected for the Pro Bowl. McNabb's winning streak continued and helped put the Eagles into the 2005 Super Bowl for the first time in 24 years. It was a record any player would be proud of regardless of his color.

And what was Rush Limbaugh doing in those months? In October, he announced that he was addicted to prescription painkillers and was headed for rehab for the third time. (Ironically, he had earlier spoken about the need to jail more drug abusers.) In December, after his return to radio, investigators found that Limbaugh was seeking doctors to prescribe such drugs as OxyContin illegally, or trying to get prescriptions from more than one doctor at a time. His lawyer said Limbaugh paid hush money to an ex-maid who kept him supplied with black-market OxyContin for four years.

Not only did Limbaugh suffer humiliation for his personal problems and his hypocrisy, he showed himself to be a football-field off the mark as a sports commentator. And McNabb showed that anyone who thought he owed his acclaim to his skin color didn't know a pigskin from a giant OxyContin tablet.

# Pulling
# the Plug

●●●

*olitically Incorrect* was the name of the late-night television show, and its host, Bill Maher, attracted a large following by fearlessly mocking religion and other sacred cows. But one week after two planes slammed into the World Trade Center, Maher made an observation that was too politically incorrect for his own good.

Noting that President Bush and others had called the September 11th terrorists cowardly, Maher remarked, **"We have been the cowards**

**lobbing cruise missiles from 2,000 miles away. That's cowardly. Staying in the airplane when it hits the building, say what you want about it, it's not cowardly."**

The White House promptly hit back. "There are reminders to all Americans that they need to watch what they say, watch what they do," said the presidential press secretary. "This is not a time for remarks like that. There never is."

Some commentators defended Maher, pointing out the difference between physical and moral cowardice. And Maher quickly apologized for his remarks, saying that they'd been aimed at political leaders, not soldiers. But with the nation still mourning the loss of 3,000 lives, the remark was too controversial for some of the show's sponsors. FedEx and Sears Roebuck pulled their commercials from the program. Some stations stopped airing the show. *Politically Incorrect* was cancelled the following June.

Still, Maher had the last laugh. A year later he came back with *Real Time With Bill Maher,* a late-night show on HBO that was as politically incorrect as its predecessor.

# The Biggest Boob

● ● ●

A stout, hard-drinking, and much-married Englishman, CBS golf commentator Ben Wright had a reputation for swinging a bit wildly at times. But he was completely out of bounds when, during the 1995 LPGA tournament, he told a reporter that women weren't cut out for golf. **"Women are handicapped by having boobs," he said. "It's not easy for them to keep their left arm straight, and that's one of the tenets of the game. Their boobs get in the way."**

What's more, he said, women's golf was "a butch game." Lesbianism on the tour "is not reticent," he was quoted as saying in a front-page article by reporter Valerie Helmbreck in *The News Journal* of Wilmington, Delaware. "It's paraded. There's a defiance in them in the last decade."

"The Boob on the Tube" was the way *The New York Post* headlined the story. Wright denounced the story as "a pack of lies," however, and CBS Sports backed him up. But Wright couldn't keep his mouth shut. He told a fellow sportswriter that he'd been accurately quoted but had been guaranteed anonymity. Then he told *Sports Illustrated* that Helmbreck was divorced, involved in a custody battle, and possibly a lesbian with a gay-rights agenda. Wright said it was his bad luck to run into her around Mother's Day, when Helmbreck was upset because she couldn't see her children. "She chose to nail me," Wright told the magazine. "She's a very unhappy woman."

Helmbreck, who was married and the mother of three, said that the entire interview was on the record, except for a small segment that she declined to reveal. *Sports Illustrated* turned up a memo that described that part of the interview. In it, Wright talked about his "fingernail test." Players with short fingernails are gay, Wright said; players with long fingernails are not.

Wright had swung himself into a pit. CBS fired him.

Years later, he expressed bitterness that he was remembered simply as someone who lost his job. "I thought I had a lot more to offer the game," he said. But among women golfers, his legend endures. In an interview with *Golf Magazine* in 2003, Jan Stephenson, a glamorous one-time golf champion from Australia, recalled Wright's observations about golfing and boobs. Laughed Stephenson, "He's got breasts as big as mine now."

# Off His Rocker

• • •

Maybe it was the three cold nights at Shea Stadium during the 1999 National League playoffs. Maybe it was the bottles whizzing over his head or the Bronx cheers from Mets fans that greeted him when he trotted out to the mound. Whatever the cause, Atlanta Braves pitcher John Rocker was clearly soured on New York.

When a *Sports Illustrated* reporter asked him how he'd feel about playing for the Mets, Rocker exploded—admittedly, not an unusual condition for the hot-tempered Georgian. "I would retire first," he said. **"Imagine having to take the [No.] 7 train to [Shea Stadium] looking like you're**

**[in] Beirut next to some kid with purple hair, next to some queer with AIDS, right next to some dude who got out of jail for the fourth time, right next to some 20-year-old mom with four kids. It's depressing."**

And that wasn't all Rocker didn't like about the Big Apple. **"The biggest thing I don't like about New York are the foreigners. You can walk an entire block in Times Square and not hear anybody speaking English. Asians and Koreans and Vietnamese and Indians and Russians and Spanish people and everything up there. How the hell did they get in this country?"**

Not surprisingly, his remarks outraged just about everybody. Rocker, then 25 years old, tried to apologize. He blamed his desire to win. "I want everybody to understand that my emotions fuel my competitive desire," he said. "They are a source of energy for me. However, I have let my emotions get the best of my judgment."

"I'm not a racist or prejudiced person," he said. "But certain people bother me."

Among the people bothered by Rocker was Braves management. He was ordered to undergo psychiatric testing, received a 14-day suspension for his comments, and was sent down to the minors for a few days. But his strong pitching arm kept him in the game until 2001, when the Braves traded him to Cleveland. From there it was back to the minors. On last report, he had been released by the Long Island Ducks—just a short train ride away from the Big Apple.

# A Lott of
# Regrets

• • •

When Strom Thurmond turned 100 at the end of 2002, he was the oldest and longest-serving senator in the nation's history. It was only natural that his Senate colleagues would hold an event to honor him, and that one of the speakers would be Trent Lott, who had served as Senate Majority Leader and was slated to reclaim the post when the Senate reconvened the next month.

Lott is a gracious speaker, but he was somewhat too facile in choosing what to praise in Thurmond's long career. In 1948 Thurmond had run for president on a State's Rights ticket emphatically opposed to civil rights and racial integration—a stand that virtually the entire country, including Thurmond himself, had backed away from over the ensuing years. But in heaping praise on the aged senator, Lott boasted that his own state of Mississippi had voted for Thurmond and that **"we're proud of it. And if the rest of the country had followed our lead, we wouldn't have had all these problems over the years."** There was an audible gasp from his audience, which included many Thurmond family members, followed by stunned silence.

Politicos and commentators across the spectrum were also stunned. Just what "problems" was Lott referring to? The "problem" of racial integration? The "problem" of equal rights? Democratic Rep. John Lewis expressed the dismay of many when he said, "I could not believe that he was saying what he said . . . . Is Lott saying the country should have voted to continue

segregation, for segregated schools, 'white' and 'colored' restrooms? . . . That is what Strom Thurmond stood for in 1948."

Republicans agreed that their Majority Leader should be more positive— or at least more discreet—in discussing the advances of the past half-century, and Lott was forced out of his leadership position. He stayed on as a senator, but only as one in a hundred—not as the mover and shaker that he had been slated to become.

# Maybe Earthbound Doctors Don't Make House Calls, But Space Docs Do

• • •

J ust about everyone loves to hear stories of people who defy the odds and survive seemingly hopeless medical conditions. But perhaps Volusia County, Florida, council member Lynne Plaskett should have refrained from discussing her miracle cure.

Plaskett appeared in a panel discussion on the Maury Povich TV show during her run for re-election in 1996. The show wasn't about political issues, though, but about alien abductions.

Plaskett said she had been diagnosed with metastatic T-cell lymphoma 20 years earlier and that her doctors had given her three months to live. The night before she was to go to New York for a last-ditch try at chemotherapy, she said, she heard a strange buzzing sound, her room filled with a fog, and she was levitated off her bed. A disc-like object came through the window, she continued, hovered over her, and scanned her body, then left the room. The next morning she knew she wasn't going to die. Within four months she was in complete remission.

Some time later, Plaskett said, she realized that her "treatment" had been courtesy of extraterrestrials who paid her a house call from their mother ship. Doctors, more mundanely, attributed the cure to drugs, chemotherapy, and her positive attitude. Nobody asked Plaskett's insurance carrier if cosmic medical treatments were covered.

Her constituents may have wished Plaskett good health, but many were reluctant to be represented by someone who claimed close encounters of the third—or any—kind. "Flakey," said one voter, "I don't vote for aliens." Plaskett lost the election to a candidate who seemed more, well, down to earth.

# Flip-Flopper

• • •

I n a long and hard-fought presidential campaign, countless factors determine how the voters decide. But according to Karl Rove, George Bush's political mastermind, one of John Kerry's fatal missteps was his hapless description of his vote on funding the invasion of Iraq. **"I actually did vote for the $87 billion before I voted against it,"** Kerry said at the first debate among Democratic contenders for the 2004 presidential nomination.

Here's what Kerry meant: He voted for a resolution that would have approved $87 billion in emergency funds for troops and reconstruction in

Iraq and Afghanistan when it was first presented as leverage to avoid war—and war would have been a multilateral last resort. That vote failed. On the key, up-or-down vote on the $87 billion itself, Kerry was one of only 12 senators to vote "no."

But forget such subtleties. Karl Rove saw a golden opportunity. Kerry's vote—and his tangled explanation—became the basis for Bush's charge that his opponent was a flip-flopper. It inspired a television ad that showed Kerry windsurfing left and right while a voiceover said the Democrat's positions shift "whichever way the wind blows . . . .

"In which direction would John Kerry lead?" the voiceover jeered. "Kerry voted for the Iraq war, opposed it, supported it, and now opposes it again. He bragged about voting for the $87 billion to support our troops before he voted against it."

In an interview on *Fox News* a few days after the election, Rove laughed about Kerry's remark. Politically, he said, "It's the gift that kept on giving."

# Fool's
# Gold

•••

I n England, when a senior executive blasts his company's products or
customers, they call it "doing a Ratner." That's in honor of an English
jeweler who dissed his product so badly that he lost not only his job but
his company as well.

Addressing the prestigious Institute of Directors in 1991, Gerald Ratner
joked that his Ratner's Jewellery store chain **"sold a pair of earrings
for under a pound, which is cheaper than a prawn sandwich**

**from Marks & Spencer, but probably wouldn't last as long."** He added, **"We also do cut-glass sherry decanters complete with six glasses on a silver-plated tray that your butler can serve you drinks on, all for £4.95. People say 'How can you sell this for such a low price?' I say, because it's total crap."**

In essence, Ratner was saying his wares were fool's gold, and his customers were fools. Enraged, they stopped shopping at his stores. Within months his company's value had fallen by an estimated £500 million. Ratner was forced off the board by investors and in 1994 his name was dropped by the company, which later renamed itself Signet.

Amazingly, Ratner staged a comeback in 2003. With funding and merchandise from an Indian jewelry manufacturer, he launched a web-only retailer, undercutting brick-and-mortar stores on prices for watches and jewelry. His initial plan was to call his site Ratners-Online because, he reasoned, "people are more likely to hit on this site than on some unknown name." Signet refused to let him use the name, however, and Ratner settled for GeraldOnline. As for the jewelry—well, would you be interested in a nice prawn sandwich?

# The Presidency: Technocrats Need Not Apply

● ● ●

Michael Dukakis, the Democratic presidential nominee in 1988, impressed most Americans as somewhat cold and unfeeling. Perhaps CNN correspondent Bernard Shaw was probing to find an emotional side of the candidate when he posed the first question of the second presidential TV debate that year.

"Governor," Shaw asked, "if Kitty Dukakis were raped and murdered, would you favor an irrevocable death penalty for the killer?"

Another candidate might have seen Shaw's unorthodox question as an opportunity to let the audience of 62 million know that he cared deeply about his wife and would be angry and distraught if such a tragedy were to strike—in other words, to "humanize" himself.

Not Michael Dukakis. "No, I don't, Bernard," he said. **"And I think you know that I've opposed the death penalty during all of my life. I don't see any evidence that it's a deterrent, and I think there are better and more effective ways to deal with violent crime."**
And on . . . And on . . . And on . . . until he had used up his allotted time.

Dukakis's bloodless and windy reply confirmed in many voters' minds that he was a callous technocrat, out of touch with his—or perhaps anybody's—emotions.

Three weeks later, they callously rejected him at the polls.

# Strike
# Four!

•••

When Marge Schott took control of the Cincinnati Reds in 1984, the wealthy widow charmed baseball fans with her lively eccentricity and her Reds-cap-wearing St. Bernard, Schottzie. But within a few years Schott was committing verbal fouls that got her thrown out of the ballpark.

First, several former Reds executives said she referred to players and business associates using racial and ethnic slurs. Then, in an interview in

1992 with *The New York Times,* Schott said, **"Hitler was good in the beginning, but he went too far."** She said she used the word "nigger" only in jest and couldn't understand why "Jap" was offensive. Later, asked if she was prejudiced against Jews, she responded, "No. They are not smarter than us, just sharper."

The baseball commissioner, Bud Selig, fined her $25,000, benched her for the 1993 season, and enrolled her in sensitivity training classes. Quipped sportswriter Rick Reilly, "Sending Marge Schott to sensitivity training is like sending a pickpocket to a Rolex convention."

Back in play, Schott soon struck out again. When an umpire suffered a fatal heart attack during the first inning of the season opener in 1996 and the game was called off, she told *The Cincinnati Enquirer,* "I feel cheated. This isn't supposed to happen to us, not in Cincinnati. This is our history, our tradition, our team. Nobody feels worse than me." She made another complimentary remark about Hitler to ESPN and spoke in a mock Japanese accent while describing a meeting with the Japanese prime minister.

Forced again to relinquish daily control of the Reds, she turned over control of the team in 1999 to business magnate Carl Lindner. When she died in 2004, Lindner told the *Enquirer,* "What was on her heart was on her tongue."

# Hale, Hale, the Spies Are all Here

• • •

Every American schoolchild learns about Nathan Hale's inspiring declaration before being hung by the British during the Revolutionary War: "I only regret that I have but one life to lose for my country." What the kids don't learn is how Hale's loose words got him to the gallows in the first place.

Operating as a spy, Hale slipped through British lines in Long Island and befriended a British officer, who informed Hale over dinner that he was a spy. **"I'm a spy, too,"** Hale bragged. Before dessert was served, armed Redcoats appeared and Hale was in terminal custody.

The moral: if you're a spy, keep quiet about it. Another moral: if you're so dumb that you need this advice, don't be a spy.

# A Weatherman Creates a Perfect Storm

• • •

Tex Antoine became a New York television weatherman in 1949 and, thanks to his charm and his upbeat, wry sense of humor, he soon became a fixture on tubes throughout the metropolitan area. In the early 1970s, he was part of a team on the WABC-TV evening news that pioneered "happy-talk news," in which the newscasters bantered and ad-libbed with each other to the delight of both audiences and the ratings-conscious station management.

But Antoine ad-libbed himself out of a job in the fall of 1976 when, following a report of an attempted rape of an 8-year-old girl, he introduced his weather report with some brazenly tasteless words of advice: **"When rape is inevitable, lay back and enjoy it."** WABC's switchboard lit up like the Rockefeller Center Christmas tree. WABC-TV management wasted no time proclaiming the obvious, that the remark was "insensitive and offensive" and "an inexcusable lapse of judgment." They also announced Antoine's suspension.

Antoine apologized and there was talk of rehiring him, but the suspension was made permanent soon afterwards. The banter on "happy-news" continued, however. Five days after the incident, anchor Roger Grimsby introduced Antoine's replacement by suggesting that viewers "lie back, relax, and enjoy the weather with Storm Field."

# Make His Day

• • •

Gregg Easterbrook had had it—up to *here*—with the way movies glorified violence. And because in 2003 Easterbrook, a senior editor at *The New Republic,* had just launched a blog on the magazine's website, he could let the world know exactly how he felt about *Kill Bill,* the newest Quentin Tarantino revenge epic.

In his blog, Easterbrook inveighed against the film's graphic violence. He concluded: **"Disney's CEO, Michael Eisner, is Jewish; the chief of Miramax, Harvey Weinstein, is Jewish. Yes, there are plenty of Christian and other Hollywood executives who**

**worship money above all else, promoting for profit the adulation of violence. Does that make it right for Jewish executives to worship money above all else?"**

It sounded like Easterbrook was trying to drive the moneylenders out of the temple, and it didn't take long for the wrath of Eisner and many other Jews to descend upon him. The Anti-Defamation League denounced him. "Tuesday Morning Quarterback," his sports column on ESPN.com, was cancelled, wiping out about half of his annual income. He suspected that it wasn't a coincidence that ESPN was owned by Disney. In fact, the word on the street was that Eisner personally was going to use his influence to punish him.

Easterbrook apologized, again and again. He admitted "stumbling into a use of words that in the past people have taken as code for anti-Semitic feelings." Holding Jewish executives to a higher standard because of the history of violence against the Jewish people was "simply wrong," he said. His friends and editors, many of them Jewish, rallied to his defense. With their help, he drafted apologies to Eisner and Weinstein. *The New Republic* issued a separate apology to its readers.

Easterbrook's efforts at damage control worked. His sports column was picked up by the National Football League's website, and he kept his Easterblogg. But he probably learned to consider his targets more carefully. As he noted during the furor, in a previous column he had speculated about the likelihood of "exaggerated gore" in Mel Gibson's *The Passion of the Christ,* which had not yet premiered. "I raised the exact same question about a Christian," he recalled, and "there was not a single peep."

# Greek Tragedy

• • •

It was a few days before the Super Bowl of 1988, and Jimmy (The Greek)—a onetime Las Vegas bookie and odds-caller turned pro football commentator for CBS—was holding forth at Duke Zeibert's, a popular Washington restaurant. As it happened, it was Martin Luther King Day.

A local television reporter asked Snyder what he thought of pro sports' civil rights record. Snyder replied that whites were holding on to coaching jobs because, with blacks dominating the playing fields, management was the only role left for them. He added that young black athletes work harder than their white counterparts.

Enlightened comments indeed. But then the Greek rolled the dice again. **"The black is a better athlete because he's been bred to be that way,"** he observed. **"During slave trading, the slave owner would breed his big black to his big woman so he would have a big, black kid, you see. That's where it all started."**

And for Jimmy the Greek, that's where it all ended. Some of Snyder's friends, including African-American colleagues, maintained that the Greek wasn't a bigot; his brother said he actually meant his remarks as a compliment. But with a *Washington Post* columnist comparing him to Nazi propaganda minister Joseph Goebbels and the NAACP declaring that his comments could set U.S. race relations back 100 years, the odds were against the Greek. Fired by CBS, he died eight years later at the age of 77, feeling bitter and misunderstood.

In fact, the Greek was not only politically incorrect, he was historically inaccurate, too. Michael Blakey, an anthropologist at Howard University, told

*The Washington Monthly* that, while plantation owners did breed their slaves, there was nothing scientific about it. "It was pure and simply a matter of reproducing large numbers rather than body types," he said. "That kind of breeding couldn't possibly lead to any difference in athletic ability."

# Bloc Head

● ● ●

During his 1976 TV debate with challenger Jimmy Carter, President Gerald Ford made a statement that left much of his audience gaping in disbelief. **"There is no Soviet dominance of Eastern Europe,"** he said emphatically, "and there never will be under a Ford administration." Ford made the remark to rebut the notion that his administration had, in effect, ceded Eastern Europe to the Soviet sphere of influence.

When the Iron Curtain fell some years later, Ford's remark would have been right on the money. But in 1976, the Soviet Union was going strong and nobody (except Ford) would question that Eastern Europe had little choice but to live in its shadow.

Ford's remark particularly stung Eastern European ethnic groups, which heard it as an expression of ignorance or a lack of concern for their homelands. Those groups were concentrated in key industrial states like Ohio, Wisconsin, and Pennsylvania, all of which narrowly went for Carter and made him the next President—and sent Ford home to write his memoirs.

# Schlock

# Jocks

• • •

Okay, radio's shock jocks are *supposed* to say awful things. In fact, a shock jock who isn't shocking would probably lose his job. But sometimes—actually, a lot of the time—a disc jockey says something so appalling that he's fired on the spot.

The vast majority of these remarks are racist, with a sprinkling of sexism, homophobia, blasphemy, and just plain vitriol. Worse still, they're not funny. And since shock jocks don't fall from particularly lofty heights—unless you think gutters are lofty—it's not especially noteworthy when they're fired. Many of them soon find work at other ratings-hungry stations willing to hire them on contracts with quick-termination clauses.

Still, sometimes a shock jock does something so, well, shocking, that it stuns even the most hardened listeners and makes national news. That's what happened in early 2005, when WQHT-FM, a hip-hop and R&B station catering to the African-American market in New York, played a song making fun of the South Asian tsunami that claimed some 220,000 lives one month earlier.

Sung to the tune of "We Are the World," the all-star charity anthem that generated millions of dollars for African famine relief 20 years earlier, the parody described "Africans drowning, little Chinamen swept away." It said God was laughing and telling victims to swim, and predicted that the orphaned survivors would be sold into slavery. The chorus, sung by a Michael Jackson imitator, said, **"So now you're screwed/It's a tsunami/You'd better run . . . go find your mommy."**

(Maybe you're not shocked? We haven't reprinted the worst of the lyrics here. Frankly, we're too shocked.)

It was an appalling performance even for WQHT, which had an impressive history of slurs against Asians and Latinos, and reaction was swift. Representatives of Asian-American and Muslim communities expressed outrage. Some New York lawmakers demanded that the Federal Communications Commission crack down on the station.

The offending radio crew apologized and offered a week's salary to relief efforts. But WQHT management, describing the song as "morally and socially indefensible," suspended the crew for two weeks and ultimately fired two of its members, including the man who wrote the lyrics. On air, a substitute DJ was soon playing a new song by Jin, an Asian-American rapper. It began, "Since when was hip-hop about being racist and ignorant, huh?"

# Conduct
# Unbecoming

• • •

By all accounts, George S. Patton was one of the most brilliant generals America has ever produced. "Old Blood and Guts," as he was called, drove his Third Army to remarkable victories over the Nazis in Africa, Sicily, France, Belgium, and Germany. Nazi generals feared him above all American field commanders. Legends surrounded Patton, fed by his colorful, bombastic personality and his conduct unbecoming to a military leader, which included cursing and slapping two soldiers hospitalized with battle fatigue. His behavior was tolerated in large part because his military brilliance was considered crucial to achieving victory.

But once the war was over, the rules changed. In September 1945 Patton talked to a reporter about conditions in Bavaria, where the military government was under his command. Too much fuss was being made over rooting out former Nazis from positions of authority, he said. He added that **"the Nazi thing is just like a Democrat and Republican election fight"** back home. The best hope for the future was in "showing the German people what grand fellows we are," he concluded.

Given the brutality of the Nazi regime and the devastating struggle that had just been waged to defeat it, many Americans weren't inclined to be as forgiving as Patton. The general's approach also directly contradicted the U.S. policy of demoting all former Nazis, including police chiefs and plant managers.

General Eisenhower promptly called Patton on the carpet and 10 days later removed him from the command of his beloved Third Army. He was

reassigned to the American Fifteenth Army, which was a paper organization devoted to documenting and studying the tactics of the war just completed. In other words, he was given a desk job.

Patton died three months after the incident from injuries suffered in an auto accident. Ironically, the U.S. became more tolerant of former Nazis soon after his death as we hastened to rebuild Germany to stand in the way of a new threat, the Soviet Union.

# Fore!

• • •

**B**y tradition, whoever wins the all-important Masters golf tournament in Augusta, Georgia, gets to order the Champions dinner the following year. So in 1997, when 21-year-old Tiger Woods smashed both age and color barriers to win the Masters, a middle-aged white golfer named Fuzzy Zoeller felt compelled to speculate upon both Tiger and the menu he'd choose.

**"That little boy is driving well and he's putting well,"** Zoeller, who'd won the Masters himself in 1979, told a television crew. **"He's doing everything it takes to win. So, you know what**

**you guys do when he gets in here? You pat him on the back and say congratulations and enjoy it and tell him not to serve fried chicken next year. Got it?"**

The Fuzz smiled, snapped his fingers and walked away. Then he turned and added, "or collard greens or whatever the hell they serve."

When CNN ran his comment, Zoeller flailed to get out of his trap. "I've been on the tour for 23 years and anybody who knows me knows that I am a jokester," he said. "It's too bad that something I said in jest was turned into something it's not." Still, he lost major endorsement deals with Dunlop and K-Mart, which had sponsored the golfer for several years running.

As for Woods's menu the next year, it was as white-bread as they come: cheeseburgers, French fries, grilled chicken sandwiches, and strawberry and vanilla milkshakes. As a former champion, Zoeller was among the guests. He ate a cheeseburger and fries. "They were delicious," he said.

# Our Friendly Neighbor to the North

•••

nternational relations were fraying at the NATO summit in Prague in 2002. The subject was supposed to be NATO's expansion, but all that U.S. President George Bush wanted to talk about was Iraq and spending more on the war against terror.

No country bristled more than Canada, which had been scaling back defense spending for decades. Francoise Ducros, the Canadian government's director of communications, summed up her view of Bush in three words:

## "What a moron!"

As it happened, Ducros was chatting with a Canadian journalist. While she wasn't named in his report, it was easy to guess her identity. Five days after delivering her verdict on Bush, Ducros quit her post, saying that the controversy was making it "impossible for me to do my job."

Prime Minister Jean Chrétien accepted her resignation reluctantly. "She may have used that word against me a few times and I am sure she used it against you many times," he told journalists. But he also dissociated himself from his aide's view of Bush. "He's a friend of mine," Chrétien declared. "He's not a moron at all."

# Ze Beega Jerk

• • •

When footloose and fancy-free Congressman Martin Hoke of Cleveland arrived in Washington, he made no effort to keep his libidinous thoughts to himself. Asked by Maureen Dowd of *The New York Times* about being a single man on Capitol Hill, Hoke replied, "I could date Marie Cantwell or Blanche Lambert—they're hot." Cantwell and Lambert, both members of Congress, gave him a cold shoulder.

A year later, after President Clinton's 1994 State of the Union address, Hoke was wired with a mike by a female producer to comment on the speech. But his comments about the producer proved more newsworthy than those about the speech. As she walked away Hoke, unaware that the mike was on, remarked in a mock accent to a colleague, **"She has ze beega breasts."**

Cleveland newspapers dutifully reported Hoke's remarks—not the kind of publicity a politician likes to see in his hometown papers. (Hoke reportedly expressed relief when an escaped murderer's killing spree knocked the story off the front pages soon afterward.)

In the next election, Hoke was lucky to run against a candidate who, as county treasurer, had recently overseen the collapse of a county bond fund and brought the county close to bankruptcy. Hoke won that one. But two years later, voters decided they could live without Hoke's tasteless braggadocio. He was defeated by former Cleveland mayor and future presidential candidate Dennis Kucinich.

# Thinking Before You Speak Is Also a Necessity

● ● ●

I f anybody could be called Mr. Baseball, it was Al Campanis. As a young man in 1943, he played for the Dodgers, and over the next 44 years served as their scouting director and vice president of player personnel. During his tenure, the Dodgers won four National League pennants and the 1981 World Series, and signed on such luminaries as Sandy Koufax and

Roberto Clemente. "He was just a great baseball man who loved the game, who obviously dedicated his life to the game," said former Dodgers manager Bill Russell. Few would argue with that assessment. And few would expect such a devoted Dodger to be abruptly thrown off the team. It took a loose racial slur on national television to do it.

On April 6, 1987, Campanis was asked to appear on a live broadcast of *Nightline* commemorating Jackie Robinson's breaking of the racial barrier in major league baseball 40 years earlier. It was an appropriate choice, particularly since Campanis had played with Robinson many years earlier in the minors.

Host Ted Koppel asked him why, after so many years as players, so few blacks were to be found in management roles in baseball. "I don't believe it's prejudice," Campanis said. **"I truly believe that they may not have some of the necessities to be, let's say, a field manager or perhaps a general manager."** Koppel, a veritable gentleman of late-night TV, gave Campanis a chance to rephrase his thoughts, but Campanis stood his ground. In fact, he made matters worse by suggesting that blacks were not good swimmers because they "don't have the buoyancy."

Amid the predictable controversy that followed, Campanis's friends insisted that he was anything but a racist, but sportswriter Roger Kahn, who was also a guest on *Nightline,* said later that the comments were "not an accident because I have heard similar things throughout all the years in baseball: 'Sure, the blacks can run. Sure, the blacks can throw. And sure, the blacks can hit. But can they think?' And this kind of racism is endemic in baseball."

Two days after the broadcast, Dodgers president Peter O'Malley fired Campanis for his remarks, an abrupt and unceremonious end to an otherwise notable career in the game.

# Bummer!

· · ·

Senator Chic Hecht of Nevada was termed a "human gaffe machine" by *The Wall Street Journal* and, by most accounts, it was a fair characterization. But he outdid himself on the Senate floor when discussing a proposal to make Nevada's Yucca Mountain the site of a repository for nuclear waste. Hecht declared emphatically that he would not permit his state to become the **"nuclear suppository"** of the nation.

The guffaws back home were louder than a slot machine delivering a jackpot, and Hecht lost the next election in a close contest. Perhaps he just wanted to protect Nevadans from weapons of ass destruction.

# Houston, We Have a Foot in Our Mouth . . .

● ● ●

In 1989, the Houston City Council was debating renaming the city's airport after Mickey Leland, an African-American congressman who had recently been killed in a plane crash in Ethiopia while on a mercy mission. **"Just as well name it 'Nigger International,'** joked long-time councilman Jim Westmoreland to someone nearby—little suspecting that his quip was being captured on tape. Westmoreland later insisted that he had said "Negro International," but voters either didn't believe him or didn't see much distinction. They voted Westmoreland out of a job in the next election, in favor of a perennial loser.

Maybe they should honor Westmoreland by naming the airport "Keep-Your-Racist-Mouth-Shut" International.

# Houston, Here's Another Foot (Texans Have Big Mouths)

●●●

Former Houston Mayor Louie Welch was a strong contender to unseat Mayor Kathy Whitmire in the 1985 election. But that was before a television mike picked up his wisecracking remedy to the city's

AIDS problem: **"Why don't we just shoot the queers?"**

The "queers" didn't appreciate Welch's healthcare "proposal." Gay activists donned T-shirts featuring a bull's eye and the slogan "You missed, Louie!"

But Louie's aim was perfect when it came to shooting his own foot. He limped to defeat in the election.

# Here's One that Didn't Happen (as Far as We Can Tell)

● ● ●

The story goes that popular New York children's radio host "Uncle Don" Carney, once wrapped up a 1930s show with a sweet song, and then, thinking the microphone was off, announced, **"We're off? Good, well, that ought to hold the little bastards."** The remark is said to have earned him an instant pink slip.

Most experts now describe this incident as an urban legend. In other words, it appears that Uncle Don said no such thing. Nor was he fired.

There is no recording to prove Uncle Don's guilt, nor any newspaper reports of the gaffe. And, in fact, Carney continued broadcasting after the alleged remark was said to have been made. Somehow, the rumor got attached to him and, to his chagrin, it never went away.

What's that? You remember hearing it yourself? Well, perhaps you were listening to a record by blooper-maven Kermit Schaefer, who produced records, books, and even a movie of "unintended indiscretions before microphone and camera." Trouble is, Schaefer is known to have hired actors to recreate audio bloopers when no actual recordings were available, without admitting it. Shaefer's blooper is not proof of Uncle Don's guilt.

Uncle Don and his friends insisted he never made the remark, and we know of no evidence to contradict his innocence.

(It's worth noting that in 1930 *Variety* wrote that another children's radio host in Philadelphia, "Uncle Wip," referred to his audience as "little bastards" in front of an open mike and was promptly fired. Again, there is no confirmation that this ever happened, nor did the Philadelphia newspapers report it. There is also a story that a 1950s Los Angeles children's personality, Captain Jet, used unkind words to describe his young audience but, again, there is no confirmation.)

# Wrong Words from a Big Monkey

●●●

H oward Cosell was the foremost TV sportscaster of the 1970s, both loved and hated for his acerbic style, his nasal, staccato voice and, not the least, his enormous ego. He had a long record of support for civil rights and African-American athletes—most notably Muhammed Ali.

But that was overshadowed in the fall of 1983 during a Monday Night Football broadcast. Commenting on Washington Redskin's receiver Alvin Garrett's catching a pass in the second quarter, Cosell blurted, **"Look at**

**that little monkey run!"** Suddenly he found himself the object of intense and unwanted controversy.

Many viewers felt that using the word "monkey" to describe an African-American was condescending and, likely, not a term Cosell would have applied to a white athlete. Rev. Joseph Lowery, the president of the Southern Christian Leadership Conference, said that Cosell's use of the word "was a slip that reflected a thought" and that it warranted an apology.

Cosell expressed regret for using the term but insisted that it was not racist and emphasized that he used the same word when playing with his grandchildren. Roone Arledge, president of ABC News and Sports said that the use of the word was "unfortunate" but was meant as an "expression of affection," not as a slur. Garrett himself said the remark didn't bother him.

But the heat and the debate continued. Cosell left the broadcast booth soon afterwards, saying that pro football had become a "stagnant bore"—certainly no thanks to himself.

# Take a Walk

• • •

Max Cleland is a wheelchair-bound triple amputee who lost his limbs from grenade injuries suffered in the Vietnam War. In 1996, he was running for the U.S. Senate in Georgia against Republican Guy Millner.

During a debate, Millner suggested that Cleland was all talk, no action. But the words he chose were insensitive, to say the least: **"Your walk says so much more than your talk."**

In a close race, Cleland pulled ahead and won.

# Watts That Again??

•••

S ay this about former Secretary of the Interior James G. Watt: He was outspoken. Environmentalists? They're "a left-wing cult dedicated to bringing down the type of government I believe in." Preserving natural resources for future generations? "I do not know how many future generations we can count on before the Lord returns." The environment? "We don't have to protect [it]. The Second Coming is at hand." Worried about the disappearance of the ozone layer? Just wear hats, sunscreen and dark glasses.

In the spring of 1983, Watt barred the Beach Boys from the upcoming Fourth of July celebration on the Washington Mall, saying that the holiday is "for the family and solid, clean American lives," not for bands that attract "the wrong element." To Watt's surprise, that element included none other than President Reagan, who declared himself and his wife Beach Boys fans. Watt was called to the Oval Office and presented with a gift of a plaster foot shot through, as by a self-inflicted bullet. Watt laughingly acknowledged his error—if not his deficiencies as a music critic—and kept his cabinet job.

Later that year, however, Watt made a comment that couldn't be dismissed with a laugh and a piece of plaster. Demonstrating a newly acquired appreciation of cultural diversity, he boasted to a business group that his coal advisory committee included "every kind of mixture you have. **I have a black, I have a woman, two Jews and a cripple. And we have talent!"**

Talk about talent! Offending so many people in so few words takes plenty!

Calls for Watt's resignation came from across the political spectrum, overwhelming the support he had enjoyed from big business, Western governors, and a long-forgiving President.

In an earlier editorial, *The New York Times* had described Watt as "an endless source of invention, much like his eighteenth-century namesake. That James Watt invented an engine that harnessed the motive power of steam. This one merely spouts off." There was no relief from the pressure this time, and within three weeks Watt sputtered out of his job.

# Rage at the Spam Machine

•••

Unwanted e-mails, like telemarketers and door-to-door salesmen of old, arouse a particularly intense rage, especially when they express views that rankle. One evening, Rachel Buchman impulsively decided to fight hate with hate. As a result, she soon joined the unemployed.

Buchman was a 25-year-old radio reporter for WHYY-FM, the Philadelphia NPR affiliate. She received regular e-mails from laptoplobbyist.com, a conservative Internet website that regularly spewed rage against gays, the United Nations, Planned Parenthood, and many other groups and institutions she valued and respected.

One evening in November 2004, she had had enough. She gave them a call and, when a machine picked up, she left this message: **"Hi, my name is Rachel and my telephone number is -----. I wanted to tell you that you're evil, horrible people. You're awful people. You represent horrible ideas. God hates you and he wants to kill your children. You should burn in hell. Bye."**

When laptoplobbyist president Chris Carmouche heard the message, he called the number Buchman had left. He discovered that it was the number for WHYY and that "Rachel" was well-known WHYY reporter Rachel Buchman. Carmouche e-mailed a transcript of Buchman's message to laptoplobbyist's 150,000 members, along with an audio clip of it.

That afternoon, an embarrassed and chastened Buchman resigned from WHYY, offering apologies "to anyone I may have personally offended." She later attributed her ill-fated telephone diatribe to "spam rage."

And why, for heaven's sake, did she leave her work number on the tape? "As a radio reporter, I leave my office phone number on machines and voicemail about 30 times a day," Buchman wrote later. "I must have been on auto-pilot." You could say that she was too good a reporter for her own good.

# Admiral, to the Rear!

• • •

From the days of George Washington, successful military leaders have enjoyed immediate fame and become strong presidential contenders. But leading soldiers in battle and leading voters to the polls are not the same. Ask Admiral George Dewey.

During the Spanish-American War of 1898, Dewey sailed his squadron of four cruisers and two gunboats into Manila Bay and sank most of the Spanish fleet there within a little more than an hour and a half, without losing a single American life. This brief and brilliant maneuver instantly gave the Philippines to the United States, established us as a major presence in the western Pacific and made us a significant global imperial power.

Understandably, this lopsided victory made Dewey a national hero of major proportions—and put his name on many short lists of presidential favorites for the upcoming 1900 election. He modestly declared himself not up to the job, but the clamor continued.

Dewey reconsidered and finally changed his mind. But did he have the "fire in the belly" that it takes to become Chief Executive? Asked by *The New York World* if he was interested in the presidency, the esteemed admiral gave an answer that was uninspiring, to say the least:

**"Since studying this subject I am convinced that the office of the President is not such a very difficult one to fill, his duties being mainly to execute the laws of Congress. Should I be chosen for this exalted position I**

**would execute the laws of Congress as faithfully as I have always executed the orders of my superiors."**

Dewey's tepid response elicited nothing short of laughter among both Democrats and Republicans. Nobody ever got elected President by pooh-poohing the job—and, odds are, nobody ever will.

Dewey's presidential hopes sank as quickly as the Spanish fleet, never to be dredged.

# But They Shoot Horses, Don't They?

• • •

O nly the most fervent abortion opponents refuse to make exceptions in cases of rape or incest. But one Louisiana state legislator took the debate a step further by suggesting that the consequences of incest might be not only tolerable but good for us.

In 1990 the Louisiana legislature was about to pass the most restrictive abortion law in the nation. Moderates sought to add an amendment that would permit abortion in the case of rape or incest or if the mother's life was endangered.

That's when Rep. Carl Gunter of Pineville weighed in with his own brand of genetic counseling. **"When I got to thinking, the way we get thoroughbred horses and thoroughbred dogs is through inbreeding," he said. With incest, he continued, "maybe we could get a super-sharp kid."**

Louisiana politicians are known to set the bar mighty high when it comes to audacity, but Gunter had vaulted over it. Some representatives were seen burying their heads in their hands.

The legislature went ahead and passed the measure, but failed to override the governor's veto. Eugenic experimentation in Louisiana would have to wait.

The following year, the National Organization for Women campaigned vigorously against Gunter. "There was nowhere I went that I didn't quote him," NOW organizer Harriet Trudell recalled more than a decade later. "That quote, I've got that emblazoned on my brain."

The quote stuck in voters' brains as well. In the next election, they dumped Gunter, preferring a candidate who didn't compare them with dogs and horses and, presumably, knew a little more about genetics.

# Offensive End

● ● ●

D efensive end Reggie White, one of the greatest players in National
Football League history, was famous for taking aim on opposing
quarterbacks. But White, who spent his best years playing for the
Philadelphia Eagles and the Green Bay Packers, took aim as well at several
other groups that weren't in the game.

Early in 1998, White was on the short list of candidates for a plum job
of commenting on NFL games on CBS Sports. Then he accepted an invitation
to address the Wisconsin State Assembly. To everybody's surprise, he used
the opportunity to insult homosexuals, whites, Native Americans, and

Asians—for that matter, just about everybody except black football players.

Homosexuality was "one of the biggest sins in the Bible," he thundered, and it would be wrong to compare the oppression of homosexuals to that of blacks. **"Homosexuality is a decision. It's not a race."** Then he offered his views of other groups. He said that American Indians couldn't be enslaved by the Europeans because they "knew how to sneak up on people. . . . White people were blessed with the gift of structure and organization. You guys do a good job of building businesses and things of that nature and you know how to tap into money pretty much better than a lot of people do around the world."

**"Hispanics are gifted in family structure,"** he continued. **"You can see a Hispanic person and they can put 20 or 30 people in one home. They were gifted in the family structure. When you look at the Asians, the Asian is very gifted**

**in creation, creativity, and inventions. If you go to Japan or any Asian country, they can turn a television into a watch. They're very creative."**

After that, CBS Sports never called. White's wife, Sara, said that CBS "wimped out" because of pressure from gay groups. "They were too scared of the Sodomite community," she opined. White, an ordained minister who was known as the Minister of Defense because he led prayers in the Packers' locker room, asserted, "I'm not backtracking on anything I said."

# It's a
# Helluva Town

●●●

I t's said that nobody reads the articles in *Playboy* magazine. But plenty
of people saw excerpts of the 17-page interview with New York City
Mayor Ed Koch it published in 1981—and the ensuing flap doomed his
short-lived run for governor the following year.

For a man who purportedly wanted to lead New York State, Koch
sounded mighty disdainful of anything north of the Bronx. Suburbia, he
said, was "sterile." Asked about the long waits New Yorkers endured for late

subways, he retorted **"As opposed to wasting time in a car? Or, out in the country, wasting time in a pickup truck? When you have to drive 20 miles to buy a gingham dress or a Sears Roebuck suit? This rural America thing—I'm telling you, it's a joke."**

Upstaters didn't find the joke very funny. *The Albany Times-Union* summed up Hizzoner's comments with this headline: "Ed Koch to Albany: Drop Dead." In the primary, New York voters returned the compliment. Although Koch had once held a commanding lead, he was trounced by Mario Cuomo, who went on to become the state's three-term governor.

Koch may have wished that New York readers of that issue of *Playboy* had looked only at the centerfold, but he didn't admit it. "I didn't want to be governor anyway," he told a reporter years later. In other words, "fuhgeddaboutit!"

# Think Again, Mr. Secretary. Perhaps They Want a Few Things Other than That.

• • •

President Gerald Ford's Secretary of Agriculture, Earl Butz, arguably set the gold standard for an offensive remark by a cabinet secretary.

He was in an airplane flying to Los Angeles after the 1976 Republican convention in Kansas City, conversing with singer Pat Boone and John Dean of Watergate fame.

As Dean later related in a *Rolling Stone* interview, Pat Boone commented that the Republicans, as the party of Abraham Lincoln, should attract more black people than they had.

"I'll tell you why you can't attract coloreds," Secretary Butz proclaimed. "Because coloreds only want three things. You know what they want?"

Boone shook his head no; so did Dean.

**"I'll tell you what coloreds want. It's three things: first, a tight pussy; second, loose shoes; and third, a warm place to shit. That's all!"**

When Dean told the tale, he identified its teller only as an unnamed cabinet member, but it didn't take the sleuths of the press much effort to find out which one. As editors grappled with how to report the secretary's language in family newspapers, the reaction among politicos and the media was fast and furious—all the more so, perhaps, because the presidential election was only a few weeks away. The self-proclaimed expert on African-Americans' aspirations was out of the cabinet faster than you can say, "No ifs, ands or Butz."

# The French Have a Word for It— Unfortunately, It's the Wrong Word

...

C oming from a diplomat, it was a singularly tactless remark. **"That shitty little country Israel"** was threatening world peace, said Daniel Bernard, France's ambassador to the United Kingdom in 2001. **"Why should the world be in danger of World War III because of those people?"**

Unfortunately for Bernard, he made those comments at a London dinner party at the home of Lord Black, then owner of *The Daily Telegraph,* a leading British newspaper, and his wife, Barbara Amiel, who is Jewish and wrote a column in the *Telegraph.* Amiel lamented in her column that anti-Semitism had become respectable at smart London dinner tables.

While Amiel didn't explicitly name Bernard, he was easily identified. A few months later he was quietly reassigned to France's embassy in Algeria where, presumably, he could safely offer his view of Israel at dinner parties.

Less than two years later, another French diplomat misspoke. At a cocktail party in Paris, Gerard Araud, France's new ambassador to Israel, described Israeli Prime Minister Ariel Sharon as "a thug" and Israel as "a paranoid country." His off-the-cuff remarks were overheard—and reported—by Boaz Bismout, the Paris correspondent for an Israeli daily.

Outraged, some French Jews and Israeli officials called for Araud's resignation. But Araud insisted that something had been lost in translation. He said that he meant that Israel has become paranoid because of what it had gone through. *Yoyou,* the word he used to describe Sharon, came under rigorous analysis. The word is sometimes used by parents of misbehaving children. However, Bismout claimed the French-Hebrew dictionary defines the word as "punk, thug, hooligan, criminal, crook."

Ultimately, Arnaud, who had served in previous diplomatic posts in Israel and was generally well-liked, kept his job. As for Bismout, he admitted that he might have violated protocol by quoting a private conversation, but said he was justified because the comments were so offensive. "What do they expect when they invite journalists to cocktails?" he wondered.

# Shoots from the Hip, Hits His Own Foot

• • •

Want to carry concealed weapons? No problem. Your style crimped by the federal ban on assault weapons? Overturn it! Those were the views of Al Salvi, a personal injury lawyer who was the Republican candidate for the U.S. Senate from Illinois in 1996.

Salvi's opponent, Democratic Congressman Dick Durbin, supported gun control and had the endorsement of James Brady, the former press secretary to Ronald Reagan who was seriously wounded during the 1981 assassination attempt on the President. Brady was a strong advocate of the bill, named after him, that would require background checks on people buying handguns. Born in Centralia, Illinois, he was also something of a local hero. Durbin made full use of Brady's endorsement, airing commercials that featured Brady and his wife Sarah and showed, in scary slow motion, a man firing an AK-47.

With one week to go before election day, Salvi returned fire. In an interview with WBBM news radio in Chicago, he asserted that "Jim Brady himself" used to deal in machine guns. At a fundraiser soon afterwards, he repeated his claim: **"Jim Brady was a licensed machine gun dealer before he was shot."**

Oops! Wrong Brady. Salvi had taken his information off the Internet, which identified a James Brady—but not *the* James Brady—as a gun dealer. "Everybody makes mistakes," Salvi said. Sure, but not everybody is forgiven. Durbin won the election in a landslide.

# The Protein
# Defense

● ● ●

After a dozen years of scouting for the minor leagues, including nine years in Asia, Bill Singer was finally back in the big leagues. The former pitcher had just signed on as a superscout for the New York Mets. Then he dropped the ball.

Bellying up to a hotel bar at a general managers' meeting in 2003, Singer struck up a conversation, of sorts, with Kim Ng, a young Asian-American woman who was the Dodgers' assistant general manager. Nothing wrong with that—except that Singer spoke to Ng in condescending, mock-Chinese accented gibberish. Two officials who were within earshot said it went like this:

Singer: "What are you doing here?"

Ng: "I'm working."

Singer: "What are you doing here?"

Ng: "I'm working. I'm the Dodger assistant general manager."

Singer: "Where are you from?"

Ng: "I was born in Indiana and grew up in New York."

Singer: "Where are you from?"

Ng: "My family's from China."

On cue, Singer delivered his nonsensical Chinese-accented gibberish. Then he asked astutely, "What country in China?"

At that point, Ng's former boss, the Yankees general manager, interrupted the "conversation." But Singer's crass behavior quickly leaked to the press, the Dodgers complained to the Mets and the Mets took Singer out of the game. He became the shortest-lived front office executive in Mets history.

Whatever he'd done—and Singer said he had no recollection—he insisted that his low-carb South Beach diet was to blame. That, and perhaps a bit too much to drink.

Could a high-protein diet really lead one to break into nonsense Chinese? "Oh, my gosh," a Harvard School of Public Health researcher told ESPN. "I've never heard that."

# Playing
# Chicken

· · ·

**J**ulia Rose is a singer/songwriter *and* a physical fitness buff. She's a free spirit with great abs. But the combination hasn't always been a boon to her career.

In 2003 Rose was performing at a Borders Books & Music store in Fredericksburg, Va., and chatting between songs. **"George Bush has chicken legs,"** she said. "He needs to pump some iron." Within a few days Rose, who had been playing gigs at Borders stores for three years, was told that her next shows in Fredericksburg were cancelled.

When a local newspaper accused Borders of censorship and people complained to corporate headquarters, Borders defended its position. In a press release, it asserted that the problem wasn't that Julia Rose had knocked Bush's legs, it was that she talked more than she sang and customers were vacating the café area where she performed. "We do not seek to take any political, social, or academic stance and certainly would not presume to take a stance on the issue of the President's legs," Borders solemnly declared.

Rose, for her part, insisted that she wasn't being partisan. "I never bashed Bush as president," she asserted. "I merely said his lower body needs some serious definition." Still, a year later she was singing a different tune. Its title: "Kerry Us Through."

# Sometimes It's What You <u>Don't</u> Say

● ● ●

Negative political campaigns go back long before 30-second TV spots. In 1884 the Republicans made sure every voter knew that Democratic presidential candidate Grover Cleveland had fathered a child out of wedlock by popularizing the ditty, "Ma, Ma, where's my Pa? Gone to the White House, ha, ha, ha!" The Democrats, also summoning the poetic muse, spread their own catchy doggerel about the Republican candidate: "Blaine! Blaine! James G. Blaine! Continental liar from the state of Maine!"

The election was decided, however, not by verse but by alliteration. At a meeting of Protestant ministers in New York six days before the balloting, Blaine listened quietly while a speaker, the Rev. Samuel D. Buchard, defined the Democrats as the party of **"Rum, Romanism, and Rebellion."** Perhaps due to a dulling of his political instincts after months of campaigning, Blaine said nothing to dissociate himself from the Reverend's bigoted association of drinkers, Catholics, and Confederates.

New York Democrats didn't miss a beat. The next day, newspapers were filled with reports of Blaine's tolerance of intolerance and fliers flooded the city's Irish neighborhoods just to make sure those most insulted were informed of his lapse. In the election, Cleveland carried New York State by a mere 1,047 votes out of over a million cast, and with it the election. No doubt, the sound of Republicans cursing was more audible than Blaine had been on the speakers' platform a week earlier.

(In case you're wondering: Had Blaine been quicker on his feet, there still would be a Cleaveland, Ohio. The city was named after a Moses Cleaveland long before Grover was born. The "a" was dropped some years later so a newspaper could shorten its masthead.)

# Whack
# Job

...

Is the Pope Catholic? D'uh! But are his priests Mafiosi?

That was the insinuation of Frank Keating, an upstanding Catholic who was selected by U.S. Roman Catholic bishops in 2002 to investigate the growing allegations of sexual abuse by priests. A former FBI agent and prosecutor as well as the outgoing governor of Oklahoma, Keating seemed ideal to head up the bishop's National Review Board. Within a year, however, he was butting heads with the Church.

In an interview with the *Los Angeles Times,* Keating said that some unnamed bishops had been behaving like the Mafia in their efforts to conceal information. **"I have seen an underside that I never knew existed,"** he said. **"To act like La Cosa Nostra and hide and suppress, I think, is very unhealthy. Eventually it will all come out."** He singled out Los Angeles Cardinal Roger M. Mahony for what he characterized as resistance to a national survey on the extent of the problem.

Father, call your *consigliere!* Comparing bishops to the Cosa Nostra, the secretive U.S. branch of the Mafia, was "off the wall," Mahony snapped back. And within days of his interview, it was Keating who was out—of his job.

In his resignation letter, Keating said he had no regrets. "Our church is a faith institution. A home to Christ's people. It is not a criminal enterprise," he wrote. "It does not condone and cover up criminal activity. It does not follow a code of silence. My remarks, which some bishops found offensive, were deadly accurate. I make no apology. To resist grand jury subpoenas, to suppress the names of offending clerics, to deny, to obfuscate, to explain away: that is the model of a criminal organization, not my church."

# One Way to Flatten Your Congressional Career

• • •

Representative Jo Byrns of Nashville, Tennessee had a lot going for him. His father, Jo Byrns Sr. had served in Congress for 27 years and had been the Speaker of the House in the early days of the

New Deal. After Jo Senior died, Jo Junior got elected to the seat, in large part because of voters' fond memories of his father. The seat should have been a safe one for years to come. But much as Byrns benefited from his bloodline, he failed to show proper respect for another official who enjoyed an even greater legacy.

Byrns showed up at a Washington reception for King George VI and Queen Elizabeth (later the Queen Mother) in 1939 wearing a $12.50 summer suit. Later, he gracelessly conveyed his impressions of the royal couple:

**"What a couple of flat tires they turned out to be."**

Byrns's wisecrack won him no friends among the many who sympathized with the British in their heroic struggle against Hitler. It haunted him during the next year's election campaign, in the midst of the London blitz, and reinforced his Independent opponent's claim that he was weak on national preparedness. In November, Byrns was defeated in a stunning upset. His political career stayed as flat as the tires he had used to describe British royalty.

Byrns's downfall foreshadowed another political career ruined by improper treatment of a British monarch. In 1983, Queen Elizabeth II (daughter of the "flat tires") was visiting San Diego when Mayor William E. Cleator briefly touched her back as he said, "This way, Your Majesty." This was a violation of a cardinal rule of royal etiquette: Never—never!—initiate physical contact with a monarch. A British tabloid headline blared "GET YOUR HANDS OFF OUR QUEEN." San Diego voters seemed to share the outrage; Cleator was defeated for reelection later that year.

# If You Call People Ethnic Names, Learn the Vocabulary First

•••

n three hard-fought campaigns for the U.S. Senate, Alfonse D'Amato bucked political trends and won election as a conservative, anti-abortion, anti-gun control Republican from liberal New York State. In 1992, he benefited from his opponent's slip of the tongue. Tired and irritable after a hectic campaign swing, Democrat Bob Abrams called D'Amato a "fascist," a remark the D'Amato campaign cast as anti-Italian. In 1998, though, D'Amato's luck ran out, thanks to his own offence against ethnic sensibilities.

Speaking to a group of Jewish leaders, D'Amato called his opponent, Congressman Charles Schumer a **"putzhead."** The Yiddish word "putz" is an impolite term for penis, sometimes used to describe a fool. It is considered a true vulgarism, which Leo Rosten cautions in *The Joys of Yiddish* is "not to be used lightly, or when women or children are around." D'Amato at first denied using the word, then insisted that it simply meant "a fool," revealing himself as both a flip-flopper and one who was ignorant of the word's true meaning.

This was not the first time D'Amato had offended constituents with words. On Don Imus's radio program, he had ridiculed Judge Lance Ito of the O.J. Simpson trial with a mock-Japanese accent. Earlier, he had suggested that GOP gubernatorial candidate Betsy McCaughey Ross sleep with Mayor Rudolph Giuliani in order to gain his endorsement. "Putzhead" wasn't D'Amato's last verbal slipup, either. Later in the same meeting with Jewish leaders, he described Congressman Jerry Nadler, who was obese, as "Jerry Waddler."

But the "putzhead" remark hurt him the most. Voters, regardless of their ethnic roots, weren't pleased at his inappropriate language, and many Jews in particular considered him a *shmegegge* (an unadmirable, petty person) for abusing their traditional language

Come November, the so-called putzhead won.

# Even a Proper Old English Word Can Get You in Trouble

• • •

Everybody knows that municipal budgets can get tight and that sometimes painful cuts are necessary. But some ways of discussing it cause more pain than others.

David Howard, an ombudsman in the Washington, D.C., mayor's office made an unfortunate word choice in discussing the constituency services budget in 1999. **"I will have to be niggardly with this fund because it's not going to be a lot of money,"** Howard, a white man, told two black co-workers.

The word "niggardly," meaning miserly, has absolutely nothing to do with race. It dates to thirteenth-century England and appears in the Bible, Charles Dickens, and at least one Supreme Court dissent. Nonetheless, to his listeners it had a nasty racist ring.

When his use of the word leaked out, Howard felt compelled to submit his resignation, and newly inaugurated Mayor Anthony A. Williams accepted it.

Then Williams found himself assaulted from all directions. Some complained that he was unfair to an upright public servant, some saw the move as pandering, some complained of excessive political correctness. And gay activists thought he should have given Howard, who was openly gay, a better chance to explain himself. Commentators cited the incident as yet another example of the ludicrous state of politics and race relations in the nation's capital.

Williams eventually admitted that he had acted "too hastily" and offered Howard his job back. Howard said he'd like to return to city government, but wanted a different job. And in the future, he said, he'd use the word "parsimonious."

# Shell-Shocked

• • •

n three decades of covering combat, from Vietnam to the 1991 Gulf War, Peter Arnett never flinched under fire. But when the U.S. invaded Iraq in March 2003, the political flak finally got him.

Arnett was in Baghdad, reporting live for MSNBC, NBC's 24-hour cable news channel. Days after the U.S. launched its invasion of Iraq, he gave an interview to Iraqi television that in the eyes of many Americans seemed to, well, lend aid and comfort to the enemy.

First, he gushingly thanked the interviewer for the "cooperation from the Ministry of Information, which has allowed me and many other reporters to cover 12 whole years since the Gulf War with a degree of freedom which we appreciate. And that is continuing today."

Arnett noted that the war was controversial in the U.S., and that widespread civilian casualties would strengthen the opposition. **"If Iraqi people are dying in numbers, then American policy will be challenged very strongly . . . . For that reason, the Pentagon keeps saying that the civilian casualties, particularly in Baghdad in the last three or four days, at the marketplaces—the Pentagon says—well, they are Iraqi missiles that land amongst the people. They keep saying that, but of course the Iraqi government says they are clearly cruise missiles that hit the population."**

Finally, he asserted, the U.S. military had been surprised by the strength of Iraqi resistance. **"Clearly, the American war planners misjudged the determination of the Iraqi forces,"** he said.

## "The first war plan has failed because of Iraqi resistance. Now they are trying to write another war plan."

From the States, Arnett instantly came under unfriendly fire. One U.S. senator said that Arnett, who was born in New Zealand but was a naturalized U.S. citizen, should be tried for treason. NBC defended him at first, saying he had given the interview as a professional courtesy. But within days, Arnett—who called the interview a "misjudgment"—was out of a job.

Not to worry. Just days after his sacking, Arnett was hired by *The Daily Mirror,* a London-based tabloid, and by Greek state television, and was reporting again from Baghdad.

# Will He Ever Eat Lunch in this Town Again?

● ● ●

Admittedly, Michael Ovitz was already having a bad year. In fact, he'd had several bad years since he left Creative Arts Agency, the powerful talent agency he'd founded, to become president of the Disney Corporation in 1995. The onetime *uber*-agent lasted only 15 months before he was fired by his former best friend, Disney chief executive Michael

Eisner, after a very public and acrimonious power struggle.

Ovitz did walk away with a cool $140 million settlement that is still the talk of Hollywood. He sank some of that money into mall development, then into a Broadway production company that quickly went bankrupt and a dead-end effort to bring an NFL franchise to Los Angeles. His next doomed venture, a talent management agency, collapsed after three years when its television business failed and investors backed out.

So the onetime king of Tinseltown was badly tarnished when he gave an interview to *Vanity Fair* in 2002. He told the magazine that he was the victim of a **"gay Mafia"** that included, among others, DreamWorks executive David Geffen. He named several other names—some (like Geffen) openly gay, others closeted or heterosexual. "It was the goal of these people to eliminate me," he said. "They wanted to kill Michael Ovitz. If they could have taken my wife and kids, they would have."

Straight or gay, Hollywood was appalled. Geffen said Ovitz's comment "makes him look like a nut." USA Chairman Barry Diller, also named by Ovitz, pronounced him "fairly rotten." *Variety* characterized the interview as an act of "public self-immolation."

Ovitz apologized for his "gay Mafia" remark, but even Hollywood—which generally forgives everything except failure—wasn't buying. He effectively disappeared from view. A recent *Variety* article noted that, tellingly, he was never seen at Spago, the chic Hollywood eatery.

After all, as one gay newspaper noted, "It's still doubtful that any self-respecting gay person would work for him again. And where does that leave you in Hollywood?"

# Don't Give Me that Old-Time Religion

●●●

Long ago, slavery was the hottest issue in America, but that was before the Civil War and the 13th Amendment changed things. Fast forward to 1996 and—guess what!—somebody thinks slavery wasn't such a bad idea after all. One Alabama state senator found justification for it in, of all places, the Bible.

**"People who are bitter and hateful about slavery are obviously bitter and hateful against God and His word, because they reject what God says and embrace what mere humans say concerning slavery."** So wrote Sen. Charles Davidson in a speech he planned to deliver in the state legislature in support of a proposal to fly the Confederate battle flag over the capitol. The measure was tabled before the speech was given, but to make sure his views were known Davidson passed out copies of the text.

Davidson cited passages in Leviticus and Timothy as proof that God felt differently about slavery than just about every American does nowadays. But Bible Belters in his area were not swayed by Davidson's reading of the Good Book. He was forced to withdraw from an upcoming congressional primary because of the furor his comments aroused.

Had he been elected, would Davidson have proposed legislation to make slavery legal again? God only knows!

# Dirty
# Laundry

●●●

George Romney was a popular three-term governor of Michigan and a leading voice of the progressive wing of the Republican party. He was the first to announce his candidacy for the 1968 presidential nomination, and was considered the frontrunner in a field that included future presidents Richard Nixon and Ronald Reagan.

The Vietnam War was the prime issue that election year. Where did Romney stand? In 1965, he had visited Vietnam, talked with American diplomats and military leaders, and announced his support of the war effort. Two years later, in a local Detroit television interview, Romney said, **"When I came back from Vietnam, I just had the greatest brainwashing that anybody can get. . . .** Not only by the generals but also by the diplomatic corps over there, and they do a very thorough job."

Critics representing Romney's rivals wasted no time raising hard-hitting questions: Could a man so easily deceived run the country? Why did it take Romney two years to discover the deception? Was he impugning the integrity of honorable diplomats and generals? And was it possible, as *The Detroit News* speculated, that Romney was "either incapable of maintaining a stand on so vital an issue or, less charitably, that he trims his Vietnam position to accommodate prevailing political whims"? Romney called a news conference to explain that his experience had not been "Russian-style but L.B.J.-style brainwashing," otherwise known as "a snow job, hogwash or news manipulation."

But the distinction was too subtle for the world of politics. Romney's support, like his brain, was all washed up. He withdrew as a candidate weeks before the first primary, leaving the way for Richard Nixon to win the nomination and the presidency.

# Off with Her Head

...

A slip of the tongue and people today can lose their careers. Two hundred years ago, they lost their heads.

In the days leading up to the French Revolution, the peasants were so famished that they rioted for bread. Marie Antoinette, wife of the unpopular King Louis XVI, heard reports of their misery. As every schoolboy knows, her flippant response was, **"Let them eat cake!"** This did nothing to endear her to her subjects, and ultimately led to the guillotine.

But did it really happen? Historians say that there is no evidence that Marie ever uttered these words or anything like them. In fact, an approxi-

mation of the phrase first appears in the *Confessions* of French philosopher Jean-Jacques Rousseau. He claimed that "a great princess" told the peasants to eat cake when she heard they had no bread. But Rousseau was writing in early 1766, when Marie Antoinette was only 10 years old and back home in her native Austria. One theory is that Rousseau coined the phrase to illustrate the gap between the royalty and the wretched poor. It's also been attributed to Marie-Therese, wife of France's Louis XIV, a century before Marie-Antoinette's time.

What's more, "let them eat cake" isn't an exact translation. According to Rousseau, the callous princess actually said, *"Qu'ils mangent de la brioche"*—or, let them eat a type of crusty bun, typically containing milk, flour, eggs, sugar, and butter. It wasn't what we'd call cake, but it was still far out of reach of the starving peasantry.

# Pin the Tail
# on the Candidate

●●●

Years before Bill Clinton met Monica Lewinsky, another politician's sexual indiscretions made headlines. It wasn't about what happened in the Oval Office but, very likely, it kept a leading contender from getting there.

On the spring of 1987, former Senator Gary Hart of Colorado was ahead in all the polls and seemed destined to become the Democratic presidential nominee the next year. Rumors of his womanizing had always followed him but, in the absence of evidence, they were just that: rumors.

Hart dismissed the allegations as distractions from the issues facing the country. Though he admitted that his 28-year marriage had been a troubled one, he denied any ongoing infidelity. In an interview with *The New York Times,* he firmly challenged nosy reporters with these words: **"Follow me around. I don't care. I'm serious. If anybody wants to put a tail on me, go ahead. They'd be very bored."**

That interview appeared in print on Sunday, May 4. Unbeknownst to Hart, reporters from *The Miami Herald,* acting on a tip, had already staked out his Capitol Hill townhouse on Friday night and seen him enter it with an unnamed "attractive blond person" who was not seen to leave the building that night. The *Herald* broke the story on the same day *The New York Times* interview appeared, making Hart appear particularly indiscreet and duplicitous.

The news of the following week was filled with Hart's denials of immoral conduct, his wife's declaration that she loved and believed him, and allegations

of more illicit romances. Hart met with his campaign staff to consider staying in the race. An aide is reported to have said, "Every time you have been seen in the past with a woman other than your wife, it's going to get printed as a story. It would be just ridiculous." In other words, forget about the issues facing the country: your flings will dominate this campaign.

On Thursday, Hart cancelled all scheduled campaign appearances, and on Friday he dropped out. The Democratic nomination eventually went to bland Michael Dukakis, whose sex life—surprise!—aroused no interest whatsoever in the national media.

(Any lingering doubt about Hart's infidelity was quashed when *The National Enquirer* ran a now-famous picture of Hart aboard a yacht called Monkey Business, with the "attractive blond person"—Donna Rice—on his lap.)

# Hasta la Vista, Señor Issel!

• • •

Dan Issel had been with the Denver Nuggets for over a quarter-century, as a star player, president, and coach. His number 44 had been retired when he stopped playing, and he was a proud member of the Basketball Hall of Fame. He might still be coaching had he not lost his cool in 2001.

The Nuggets had just lost a tight game with the Charlotte Hornets 99-96, their fifth straight loss for a total of 14 defeats out of 21 games. To make matters worse, their leading scorer had just gone public with his demand to be traded, saying he was tired of losing. Issel was on his way to the locker room after the game when an Hispanic fan taunted him over the team's poor showing. His nerves no doubt frazzled, Issel responded by yelling, **"Hey, go buy another beer! Go drink another beer, you fucking Mexican piece of shit!"** Bad enough that he shouted it, but worse for Issel that the insult was captured on tape by Denver's KUSA-TV. The station aired the footage that night and Issel was deep in hot salsa.

Two days later, Issel gave a tearful apology, describing his comment as "unchristian-like." The management announced that he would be suspended without pay for the next four games. Hispanic spokespeople thought that Issel should be fired altogether, but general manager Kiki Vandeweghe said that the suspension was severe enough. "This guy has given his whole life to this organization," Vandeweghe said. "We did not think that throwing away 25 years invested in this league and this team was warranted. Do you forget about 25 years of service over five seconds?"

The answer was yes. Two weeks later, under continuing pressure, Issel was forced to resign. To our knowledge, no beer company has asked him to endorse its product.

# Praise <u>My</u> Lord and Pass the Ammunition

•••

Soldiers obey their superiors' orders. But Lt. Gen. William G. Boykin was evidently answering to a higher authority in 2003 when he reiterated that, in the war against Muslim terrorists, Jesus was on America's side. Usually dressed in his Army uniform, Boykin, a deputy undersecretary of defense for intelligence, offered his views in Baptist or Pentecostal churches.

He told congregations that radical Islamists hate the United States "because we're a Christian nation, because our foundation and our roots are Judeo-Christian." He declared that "the enemy is a guy called Satan" and that divine intervention had put President Bush in the White House. "The majority of Americans did not vote for him," Boykin noted. "He's in the White House because God put him there for a time such as this."

Theologically speaking, it seemed, size really did matter. Recalling his role in combat in Somalia in 1993, during which his troops captured a Muslim warlord, the three-star general said, **"I knew my God was bigger than his. I knew that my God was a real god and his was an idol."**

Boykin's remarks drew fire from Muslim civil rights organizations, interfaith groups, and several members of Congress, all of whom called for his removal to a less sensitive post. "A few more of these [speeches] and Osama bin Laden won't need to make videos anymore," *Newsweek* opined.

"He can just put together the greatest hits of Boykin [and other fundamentalist Christians] and they will make his point nicely—that Americans see all Muslims as enemies."

The remarks were embarrassing to the White House, which had often described Islam as a "peaceful religion" and insisted that the war against terror was not a war against any religion. But even after a Pentagon investigation concluded that the general had violated regulations by talking out of turn, the Administration decided to let Boykin stay. Boykin, for his part, stopped speaking in churches.

# Spilling
# the Beans

●●●

How could jelly beans get anybody into trouble? Yet some comments about black jelly beans spelled early retirement for a top Texaco executive.

In 1994 the oil giant was being sued by some 1,500 African-American employees. The suit accused the company of racial discrimination in hiring and promoting, and sought more than $500 million in damages. At a meeting that summer, Texaco's treasurer Robert Ulrich discussed the lawsuit with

Richard Lundwall and a few other company executives. Unbeknownst to the others, Lundwall had a microcassette recorder in his pocket. (He said he routinely taped such meetings.)

Later, after Lundwall had been laid off and was looking for a lawyer to file an age-discrimination suit against Texaco, he handed the tapes to one of the attorneys representing the black employees.

In the initial transcription, the executives seemed to be talking about shredding documents relating to the racial discrimination case. Worse still, they sounded blatantly racist. On a closer hearing, the alleged racism took on a more innocent—but still ambiguous—tone:

First, the Texaco executives talked about those jelly beans.

**"I've heard that diversity thing, we don't have black jelly beans or green . . ."** Ulrich began.

**"That's funny. All the black jelly beans seem to be glued to the bottom of the bag,"** said Lundwall, laughing.

**"You can't have just 'we' and 'them.' You can't have black jelly beans and other jelly beans . . . . It doesn't work,"** said Ulrich.

**"But they're perpetuating the black jelly bean . . ."** said Lundwall.

Then the men discussed the holidays and diversity. Ulrich said, **"I'm still struggling with Hanukkah and now we have Kwanzaa; I mean, I lost Christmas, poor St. Nicholas, they shitted all over his beard."**

After the tapes were released, civil rights leaders called for a boycott of Texaco, outraged customers cut up their Texaco credit cards, and some investors sold their stock. In his defense, Ulrich insisted that his reference to jelly beans was prompted by a talk given by an African-American consultant at a conference he'd attended before the ill-fated meeting. The speaker had used jars of multi-colored jelly beans to illustrate racial diversity and integration.

Still, the lawsuit put Texaco in a tight spot. The company fired one of the executives at the meeting, suspended another, and cut off the retirement benefits of both Lundwall and Ulrich, who by then had also left the company.

The government indicted both Lundwall and Ulrich for conspiring to hide or destroy company documents in the racial discrimination suit. Both men were acquitted in 1998. As for the discrimination suit, Texaco agreed to a $175 million settlement with its African-American employees—and promised to expand its diversity training.

# All the News
# that Fits and
# Some that Doesn't

● ● ●

I n the pre-computer era, people who wanted to bad-mouth their employers clustered around the water cooler and griped. These days they write blogs. That, at least, was the route taken by Daniel P. Finney, a staff writer for *The St. Louis Post-Dispatch.*

Writing under a pseudonym, Finney, 29, took potshots at the newspaper and his co-workers. Close to Christmas, he grumbled about working on a "hideously lame story involving Santa Claus." On December 2, he wrote,

**"I've been reading the *Post-Dispatch*'s annual 100 Neediest Cases stories. The bottom line is that there are a lot of poor people who need stuff. It is a worthy cause. And at some level, I feel sorry for these people. But at another level . . . I must admit that I feel as if a good number of those needy cases could be avoided by a well-placed prophylactic."**

In his day job, meanwhile, Finney was writing the very pieces he disparaged in his blog. A week after sniping at the *Post-Dispatch* series, a "100 Neediest Cases" article appeared under his byline.

Although the blog was fully accessible in cyberspace, it wasn't until an excerpt appeared in an alternative newspaper that newsroom management paid attention. At that point, it seized Finney's hard drive and suspended him from reporting duties. A week later, having taken down his blog, he resigned.

# That Championship Season

• • •

Sometimes rape victims take the blame because they dressed seductively. Sometimes they're blamed because in the past they've slept around. But can a rape victim be blamed because she was a bad football player?

That was the suggestion of University of Colorado football coach Gary Barnett. In 2004 Katie Hnida, who had been a place-kicker for the Buffaloes a few years earlier, told *Sports Illustrated* that she had been raped by a teammate in 2000. She came forward after about a half-dozen other women also said that they'd been raped by UC football players or recruits.

Speaking to a group of local reporters, Barnett said that, in a sense, Hnida had it coming. **"It was obvious Katie was not very good,"** **he said. "She was awful. You know what guys do? They respect your ability. You can be 90 years old, but if you can go out and play, they respect you. Katie was a girl and not only was she a girl, she was terrible. OK? There is no other way to say it."**

Barnett was promptly suspended, but not without full pay. But at some schools, football is everything. UC's athletic director resigned under pressure but Barnett—despite his remarks, the other allegations of rape, and an independent investigation that found that drugs, alcohol, and sex were used to entice recruits—was soon reinstated. He went on to have a winning season. At the end of 2004 he was named Associated Press Big 12 Coach of the Year after leading his team to the conference title game. In fact, he outlasted the university president, who stepped down in 2005 as the football scandal snowballed.

And Hnida, who had transferred to the University of New Mexico, showed the Buffaloes she wasn't so awful after all: She became the first female kicker to score in Division I college football.

# In the Soup

●●●

Soupy Sales probably had more pies thrown in his face than any other TV personality. His children's show with its rapid-fire slapstick, bad puns, and general goofiness appealed to audiences of all ages. He had a reputation for making thinly veiled off-color jokes on the air ("What starts with 'f' and ends with u-c-k? A fire truck!") but he flatly denied ever having made such jokes on camera, nor could anybody prove that he had. But he couldn't deny his ad-libbed remarks at the end of his New Year's morning show in 1965 which, though not off-color, got him pulled off the air as quickly as if they had been.

**"Hey kids, last night was New Year's Eve,"** Soupy said, "and your mother and dad were out having a great time. They are probably still sleeping and what I want you to do is tiptoe in their bedroom and go in your mom's pocketbook and your dad's pants, which are probably on the floor. You'll see a lot of green pieces of paper with pictures of guys in beards. Put them in an envelope and send them to me at Soupy Sales, Channel 5, New York, New York. And you know what I'm going to send you? A postcard from Puerto Rico!"

Urging kids to get their parents to part with money to buy things is one thing. Asking them to bypass the middleman and just send in their parents' money—forget the product—is quite another. The station was flooded with phone calls from irate parents who saw no humor in Soupy's prank, and his show was promptly suspended. After two weeks, the furor had subsided and he was back on the air, where he stayed for another two years.

It's not known how many "green pieces of paper with pictures of guys in beards" arrived in Channel 5's mail room.

Soupy has been making brief appearances on TV and radio ever since— and presumably being paid by check.

# Fear the Greeks, but Watch Out for the Serpents, Too

• • •

Saying the wrong thing at the wrong time can be ruinous. But so can saying the right thing at the right time. A prime example comes from one of the best-known tales of Western literature.

In ancient times, the Greek army surrounded and besieged the city of Troy for 10 grueling years, with the gods shamelessly playing favorites among the combatants. The Greeks were on the verge of calling it quits and heading home when their best soldier, Odysseus, had an idea: Build a large wooden horse, put some soldiers in it, leave it outside Troy's city walls as a "tribute," and feign a retreat. The plan was daring, but worth a try. One morning soon afterwards, the surprised Trojans awoke to find an intriguing wooden horse outside their city walls, and not a Greek in sight. Thinking they had won the war, they prepared to wheel their trophy into the city.

From our hindsight of a few thousand years—and having seen the movie—we know that admitting the horse without a proper security scan was not terribly bright, but the Trojans were eager to believe that their arch-enemy had no motive but benevolence. Then, out came Laocoon, a priest in Apollo's temple, shouting the obvious: **"Are you mad? . . . Do you think the foe has gone? Do you think gifts of the Greeks lack treachery? . . . I fear the Greeks, even when bringing gifts."**

Laocoon threw a spear at the horse and a moaning sound came from within, but—remarkably—nobody was ready to cut the creature open to find its source. Still, some Trojans suggested listening to Laocoon. Then two horrible serpents suddenly appeared, "their burning eyes suffused with blood and fire, their darting tongues licking their hissing mouths." Who do they head for? None other than Mr. Common Sense, Laocoon. The serpents wasted no time crushing him and his two young sons to death while his kinsmen looked on in horror.

The Trojans quickly concluded that Laocoon's grizzly fate was his divine punishment for spearing the horse, which must therefore be a sacred object. They blew off his advice and brought the statue into their city. That night, with the Trojans drunk out of their minds from celebrating their supposed victory, the Greek soldiers crawled out, opened the city gates to the rest of their army and Troy was soon rubble. Laocoon would have been able to say "I told you so!" to his countrymen had he not predeceased them all.

The serpents were, of course, sent by a god—how else would they know whom to crush, where, and when?—but it was a god allied with the Greeks, determined to shut Laocoon up so the Greeks could do to Troy what the snakes did to him.

The Trojans set an early gold standard for those who bring bad fortune upon themselves. And straight-talking Laocoon set one for all whistleblowers to follow. His words, though fatal, were one of the few commendable "slips of the tongue" in this book.

# About
# the Authors

**Joel Fram** was the proprietor of Eeyore's Books for Children in New York City for nineteen years. He is a co-author of *I Heard it Through the Playground: 616 Best Tips from the Mommy and Daddy Network for Raising a Happy, Healthy Child from Birth to Age Five.* He currently lives in the Philadelphia area, where he operates a small business that exports American books.

**Sandra Salmans** is a Philadelphia-based freelance writer. She is a co-author of a humor book, *The Working Mother's Guilt Guide: Whatever You're Doing, It Isn't Enough.* Previously, she was a staff reporter for *The New York Times* and a writer for *Newsweek.* She continues to freelance for the *Times.*